a guest giving way like ice melting
thirteen ways of looking at laozi

a guest giving way like ice melting

thirteen ways of looking at laozi

steven schroeder and debby sou vai keng

Library of Congress Control Number: 2010924338
ISBN: 978-0-9824405-7-5
© Steven Schroeder and Sou Vai Keng, 2010
cover design by Jess Chan Sau In

Ink Brush Press
inkbrushpress.com
Manufactured in the United States of America
Temple, Texas

Acknowledgments

"a guest giving way like ice melting 3" was first published in *The Cresset*. Thanks to my Asian Classics students for your patience and insight while I worked through these variations. Thanks to Alan Berecka, David Breeden, Jerry Craven, Paul Friedrich, Kit Kelen, Liang Huichun, Long Xiaoying, Katia Mitova, and Wang Hao for your encouragement and criticism on this project. And thanks especially to Sou Vai Keng, always an inspiration—happy to be side by side. (SS)

Thanks to Steven Schroeder for letting me wander with you and laozi in search of nothing. (SVK)

Special thanks from both of us to Jess Chan Sau In for the cover design.

This collection began as a translation of the eighty-one poems that comprise the book of Laozi known as *Daodejing*. But in its present form it is not a translation. I begin with Chinese words attributed to Laozi, but my intent is to make poems of them that work in English as ways of seeing. That the collection breaks into thirteen ways invites a passing reference to a philosophical poem of another philosophical poet intent on the plain sense of things—the blackbird among them, but also Laozi, a character inseparable from the book of characters that bears his name in a world of words to the end of it.

Books are strange—solid collections of solid things lying lifeless before us. Shine a light on them and they cast shadows that could make us mistake them for walls. But with a guide like Laozi, we might come in time to suspect that they contain nothing—and that nothing makes them work.

With regard to Laozi, I find I have nothing to say—and that saying it can be nothing other than poetry, a door if it works, through which we might pass one way or another with Laozi to other ways of seeing.

SS

1

of many minds
like thirteen blackbirds
in three trees with nothing
to say, saying
nothing. no
one

one gives rise to two
two gives rise to three
three gives rise to ten thousand
things. never mind
be

a dark door on many wonders

2

of thirteen minds
in three trees
only one free

black bird in one
rises through
one dark door

to nine folds of nothing
saying
in one song

for three thousand years
nothing
about many things

3

free

nothing
but one perching
blackbird in ten thousand

who takes wing
unafraid when
the bough gives way

a dark door
singing wonder
in ten thousand songs

4

one
unafraid
always a peer
peering in under sun
wonders of living
dancing
free

5

unafraid

one
wondering
dances
free

6

one

7

SS/SVK

contents

empty	15
sidetracked	17
walking on water	21
nothing doing	25
never mind	28
dwelling not dwelling	30
as if the world lived in it	32
a guest giving way like ice melting	38
ordinary	43
like a tasty little stir-fry	48
acting like an executioner	53
no claim	54
like a necklace of stones	56

empty

dao is
empty

bend
the edge

loose
the knot

clear as
day

it is
as though

it is
before

it was

sidetracked

1

a road is a road is a road
name named *name* – strange

nothing named *world*
begins – nothing

a name and then ten
thousand things

desire nothing
see wonders

desire wonders
see nothing

two spring
from one

say dark dark dark
say dark again

dark door on
many wonders

2

a road may go left
a road may go right

it does its work
but has no reputation

it may be called small
it may be called big

because it does not act big
it can do big things

3

one who tiptoes
does not stand

one who strides
does not walk

one who is self-conscious
does not know

one who is conceited
is not noticed

one who flatters himself
accomplishes nothing

one who boasts
does not endure

4

if I have any sense
my only concern will be
to walk on the main road

the main road is easy
but people love
to be sidetracked

the palace is spotless
but the fields
are full of weeds

the granaries are empty
but they
wear fine clothes

sated with food and drink
they have
more than they need

this is not the way
it is robbery

walking on water

1

water makes its place
in the place that is
despised

it is on
the right track

2

dwell on good earth

think deeply
act kindly
speak truly
govern justly

move in good time

no fight
no blame

3

though it is simple and small
none can grasp the nameless way

if governments could harness it
the whole world would be their guest

heaven and earth would embrace
and sweet dew would settle

the people would need no orders
all would follow their natural course

if we know when to stop
we are in no danger

like a river in a valley
flowing down to the sea

4

the ocean can rule a hundred rivers
because it is good at lying low

5

nothing in the world is
weaker than water

but nothing
can surpass it

weak overcomes strong
soft overcomes hard

the world knows this
but does not act on it

straight talk seems inside out

nothing doing

1

not being
worth a thing
means nothing

to fight about
nothing to fight about
means nothing to steal

nothing happens
when you have nothing
under control

2

wheel is made of thirty spokes
but nothing makes it work

pot is made of clay
but nothing makes it work

a door is chiseled in a room
and nothing makes it work

profit comes from what is there
but nothing makes it work

3

everything in the world is
born of something

something is
born of nothing

never mind

1

creating not possessing
doing not presuming
leading not ruling

the saint has no mind
because mind is
common

2

cultivated in the self
virtue is real

cultivated in the family
virtue overflows

cultivated in the village
virtue grows

cultivated in the nation
virtue is plentiful

cultivated in the world
virtue is universal

3

one who is full of virtue
is like a newborn

she cries all day
but does not grow hoarse
this is perfect harmony

4

do not do
serve not serve
taste not taste

great small many few
reply to blame with virtue

in hard see soft
in large see small

the hardest tasks
start easy

the wise person
does nothing
to be big

5

the good warrior is not warlike
the good fighter is not angry
the good victor is not hostile

the good commander is humble
this is using people's strength
this is the virtue of nonviolence

dwelling not dwelling

1

good walk
no tracks

good talk
no disgrace

good count
no tally

good gate
no lock

yet no one
can open it

good tie
no knot

yet no one
can loosen it

2

everyone knows beauty
as beauty because

there is something
they despise

good as
good because

not good is –
having not

having hard
easy long

short high
low sound

voice front
back one

after the other
do nothing

ten thousand
things come and go

give birth
there is nothing

working not dwelling not
dwelling does not pass away

as if the world lived in it

1

the wise
pull back
and get ahead

seek
nothing
gain more

2

better to stop at full
than to pour more

a blade honed
too fine

will not last
fill a house

with treasure
and no one can

protect it
retire when

your work is done

3

breathe
soft as a baby

be the woman
at heaven's gate

create, do not possess

4

devote your life
to the world
as if the world
lived in it

love the world
for the sake of life
and you can be
trusted with it

5

be the stream of the world
be the stream of the world
become a child again

be the rule of the world
be the rule of the world
become limitless again

be the valley of the world
be the valley of the world
become plain again

the master tailor does not cut

6

the world can not be governed
the world can not be held
to hold it is to lose it

7

one who knows
what will suffice
will not be humiliated

one who knows
when to stop
will endure

8

lose and lose and lose again
let nothing matter

nothing for nothing
nothing not for nothing

one cannot take the world on busy

9

what is tranquil
is easy to hold

what has not taken place
is easy to plan for

what is brittle
is easy to break

what is tiny
is easy to scatter

deal with it before it happens
put it in order before it is disordered

a tree big as an embrace grows
from a shoot small as the tip of a hair

a terrace nine stories tall
rises from a pile of dirt

a journey of a thousand miles
begins when you put your foot down

to act is to bow
to grasp is to lose

so the wise person doesn't act
and is not defeated

doesn't grasp
and is not mastered

the wise person
desires not to desire

learns not to learn
and dares not do

10

words have an ancestor, action
the wise person wears rough cloth
and keeps his jade in his heart

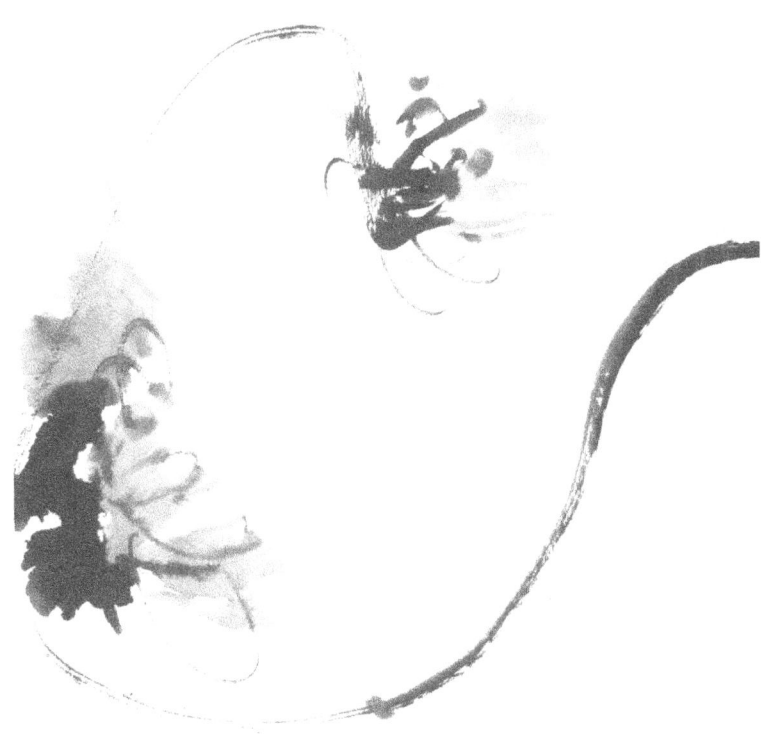

a guest giving way like ice melting

1

a mysterious woman this
door we call the world

a silk veil used
not used up

2

looking not
seeing say
formless

listening not
hearing say
faint

grasping not
holding say
subtle

these three
failed ways
to know

blend into one
no light above
no shadow below
form of no
form—image of no
image—meet it see no

beginning—follow it see no
end—grasp the ancient dao
for the sake of now

3

all we can
describe is
appearance

careful as one
who crosses
a bridge in winter

alert as one
who anticipates
danger

courteous as one
who is a guest
giving way

like ice melting –
simple as
a block of wood

open as a valley
murky as
a puddle of mud

wait while
the mud settles
wait while

the puddle clears
be still until
right action begins

not desiring
to be full
you can hide

you can become new

4

something undefined
born in the silence
and emptiness

before the world was

stands alone and does
not change

walks everywhere and is
not in danger

it could be
the mother of the world

5

forced to name it
I call it *great*

great means flow
flow means far
far means return
dao is great
heaven is great
earth is great
the people are great

these are the four powers

the people among them
the people follow earth
earth follows heaven
heaven follows dao
dao follows what is

6

those that know
don't tell

those that tell
don't know

stop talking
shut the door

untangle
the confusion

ordinary

1

empty to the limit
mind still

ten thousand things
combine and combine again

things grow
return to their roots

return to stillness
stillness is

return to life
return

to life is
ordinary

no body
no danger

2

go slow
value words

when work is done
everyone says *it was I*

3

infrequent speech is natural
a gale doesn't last all morning
a squall doesn't last all day

on the way be one with the way
succeeding be one with success
failing be one with failure

one with the way
the way is happy
one with success
success is happy
losing lose happily

trusting, trusted

4

dao does nothing
and yet there is nothing
it does not do

if governments could harness it
all beings would change naturally

if change gave rise to desire
they would be composed
with unknown simplicity

composed with unknown simplicity
they would not desire

at peace without desire
the whole world
would make itself whole

5

wise scholar
hears dao
and walks it

so-so scholar
hears dao
and can take it or leave it

poor scholar
hears dao
and laughs out loud

if there were no laughter
dao would not be
what it is

6

the beginning of the world
is the world's mother

know the mother
know the child

guard the mother
keep the body safe

stop talking
shut the door

life is full
without a care

start talking
get busy

life is
beyond hope

see small
speak clear

guard gently
speak powerfully

use light
turn and turn again

to clarity

like a tasty little stir-fry

1

weapons are
inauspicious tools
all despise them

weapons are
inauspicious tools
do not use them

victory is
not beautiful

beautify it
and you are
happy with murder

when people are killed
they should be mourned

when a victory is won
treat it as a funeral

2

don't use weapons
to conquer the world

master a place
weeds sprout

after armies pass
times are bad

get good results
that is all

get results don't
dwell on them

get results don't
cut others down

get results don't
be arrogant

get results don't
struggle

3

governing a great nation
is like a tasty little stir fry

attend to the world
and evil will have no power

4

I have three treasures

first is compassion
second is thrift
third is not daring
to be ahead of the world

compassion makes me brave
thrift makes me generous
not daring to be ahead of the world
makes me a most useful tool

abandoning compassion to be brave
abandoning thrift to be generous
giving up being last to be first
would be to die

compassion wins every fight
it is a sure defense
heaven help us
use compassion

5

small nation
few people

let there be tools
that are not used

let the people
contemplate death

let them not travel far

though there are boats and carriages
they have no use for them

though they have armor and troops
they do not display them

let people return
to the knotting of ropes

their food pleasant
their clothes pleasing
their homes safe

happy with their customs
they live within sight of

the country next door
they hear each other's
chickens and dogs

people die in old age
with no going to and fro

acting like an executioner

if people are not afraid to die
why threaten them with death?

there is an official executioner

acting like an executioner
is like playing at being a carpenter
play at being a carpenter
and you are sure to hurt your hand

no claim

1

exit life
enter death

three in ten are
disciples of life

three in ten are
disciples of death

three in ten are
living people moving
into the domain of death

those who take life in
and guard it well
can walk the path
and not meet rhinos or tigers
engage armies and not be wounded

rhinos have no place to sink their horns
tigers have no place to sink their claws
soldiers have no place to sink their swords
because they have no place for death

2

the wise person is not sick
because she is sick of sickness
sick of sickness, she is not sick

3

resolve a quarrel and
some complaint
must remain

what's the good of announcing resentment?
what's the good of believing a lie?

the wise person keeps her part of the bargain
but lays no claim on others

like a necklace of stones

1

put up a good sign
and the world will come

be beyond harm
quiet and peaceful

passing guests will stop
for music and good food

when dao speaks
it is tasteless

we look and don't see
we listen and don't hear

but it is never exhausted

2

to be interested in reputation
is to have no reputation

don't jingle like jade
don't clatter like a necklace of stones

Sou Vai Keng (Debby Sou) is a writer and painter from Macau. Sou writes novels, poetry, short stories and drama scripts in both Chinese and English. Published books include *Different Skies* (Chinese novel with illustrations, co-written with Chan Sau In), *Take a Break* (collection of ink paintings with poetry in English and Chinese) and *Everybody Has a Pet* (book of poetry in English). Her acrylic and ink paintings have been exhibited in Macau, Mainland China, the US and France.

Steven Schroeder received his Ph.D. in Ethics and Society from the University of Chicago in 1982. He is the co-founder, with composer Clarice Assad, of the Virtual Artists Collective (a "virtual" gathering of musicians, poets, and visual artists—vacpoetry.org), which has published five full-length poetry collections each year since it began in 2004. He teaches at the University of Chicago in Asian Classics and the Basic Program of Liberal Education for Adults and at Shenzhen University in China. His work has appeared or is forthcoming in *After Hours, AmarilloBay, Cha: An Asian Literary Journal; Concho River Review,* the *Cresset, Druskininkai Poetic Fall 2005, Georgetown Review, Karamu, Macao Closer, Mid-America Poetry Review, Poetry East, Poetry Macao, Rambunctious Review, Rhino, Shichao, Sichuan Literature, Texas Review, TriQuarterly* and other literary journals. He has published two chapbooks, *Theory of Cats* and *Revolutionary Patience*, and four full-length collections, *Fallen Prose, The Imperfection of the Eye, Six Stops South*, and *A Dim Sum of the Day Before*.

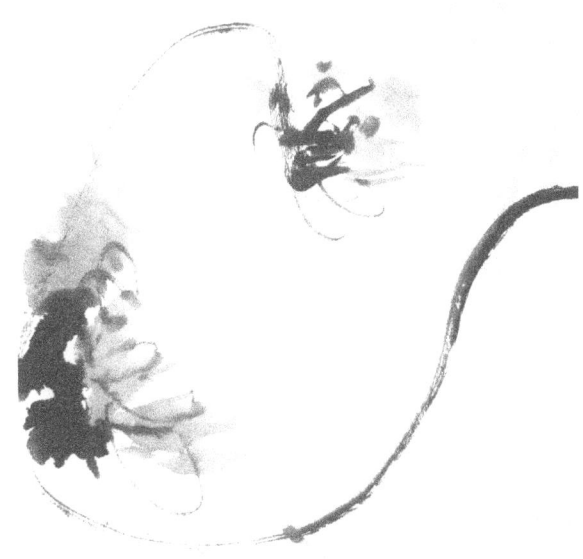

www.ingramcontent.com/pod-product-compliance
Lightning Source LLC
Chambersburg PA
CBHW031216090426
42736CB00009B/934